CW00747251

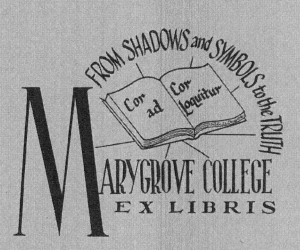

ROSEMARY SUTCLIFF

ROSEMARY SUTCLIFF

Rosemary Sutcliff

Margaret Meek

A WALCK MONOGRAPH
GENERAL EDITOR: KATHLEEN LINES

HENRY Z. WALCK, INCORPORATED
NEW YORK

For
Richard

Library of Congress Catalog Card Number: 62-18332
© The Bodley Head Ltd 1962
First American Edition 1962
Printed in Great Britain

CONTENTS

A Note about the Author

Margaret Meek is Scottish and went to school in Fife and then to Edinburgh University to read English. After teaching for two years in a finishing school, she spent some time abroad, and then returned to England to take her teacher training at Maria Grey College. Afterwards she taught at Haberdashers' Aske's Girls' School for five years before taking up a Fellowship in Education at Leeds University. Since 1955 she has been a Lecturer in Education at Bristol University.

Miss Meek is particularly interested in what children read because she feels this is of enormous importance to teachers at every stage. She and her colleagues have found that students in the Education Department at Bristol are not normally inclined to read children's books after emerging from a degree course, but that when they are encouraged to do so, they immediately have a completely different awareness of a child's world and his imagination, and are surprised to find that writing for children is a genuine art.

1. The Artist

The reputation of an author of books for children is inextricably bound up with the critical judgment of adults. Children enjoy, discriminate amongst, or reject the books which come their way, but of the two thousand or so titles which appear every year they can read only a fraction. Yet they have their avowed favourites amongst authors and their enthusiasms for particular subjects. No one who is concerned about what they read can ignore their response to what is provided, but it is well known that if no good book is available, they will read an indifferent one. It is not the young reader who will decide if a manuscript is to become a book, and although the author's success must ultimately depend on his being acceptable to the younger generation, he must first survive the judgment of his own contemporaries.

It was a wise and intuitive editor who saw promise in a collection of legends which reached the Oxford University Press after having been, as Miss Sutcliff says, 'passed from hand to hand at a regimental dinner', and commissioned her first book, *The Chronicles of Robin Hood*, which appeared in 1950. This book marked the beginning of the career of an author who has acquired a notable and distinctive reputation, based on the acclaim of children and adults alike. In the short space of twelve years Rosemary Sutcliff has written fifteen books for children, two adult novels, a book on *Houses and History* and a monograph in this series.

The intention of this essay is to review the particular excellence of Miss Sutcliff's work, especially in her historical novels for children, and to discuss the distinctive features which set her apart from even her most successful contemporaries. Miss Sutcliff would rather discuss her novels than herself. Certainly her personality emerges strongly in the themes of the books, especially the later ones. Nevertheless, all readers share the same curiosity to know something of the life of a living author and how the books are made. More especially teachers of history, who now realize that the historical novel can be their strongest ally in their attempts to convey to the young the essential continuity of history, are intrigued by the way an author invests the source material with imaginative life. In the following pages we shall see that Rosemary Sutcliff is a storyteller for whom the past is a vivid extension of the present.

Rosemary Sutcliff was born in 1920. As her father was a naval officer, for the first ten years of her life she and her mother followed him to various stations, including Malta, until he retired and the family settled in North Devon. Since the age of two, Miss Sutcliff has suffered from Still's disease (a cramping poly-arthritic condition contracted by children) which has restricted her physical movement. Her schooling was consequently erratic; she had lessons with her mother, went to school when she was nine, and left 'mercifully early' at fourteen. She educated herself thereafter. She trained as a painter at Bideford School of Art and became an expert professional miniaturist. She was a member of the Royal Society of Miniature Painters and her work has been shown at the Royal Academy. When she was twenty-five she gave up painting and began to write because, she says, she found her painting 'was becoming more of an exercise than an art'. Writing was 'more satisfying'.

One is bound to mention Rosemary Sutcliff's misfortune in order to emphasize the quite remarkable qualities of her personality in which courage and will power are dominant. Heroically independent, she is without the slightest trace of invalidism. Despite the lack of experiences common to other children, she has made the intensity of her greatest childhood joy the root of her adult achievement, and the skill acquired in her first work as an artist has fertilized the later harvest of the books. For instead of regular lessons, she had read to her by her mother an endless succession of fairy tales and legends, and the works of authors who were of especial significance to the sensitive, imaginative child: Kipling, especially in the *Jungle Books*, *Just-So Stories* and *Puck of Pook's Hill*, Whyte Melville and Kenneth Grahame. These authors fired her imagination and peopled her inner world. The surrounding landscape, denied to her as a playground, sharpened her powers of observation, which were refined to a pitch of Keatsian sensibility in response to the changing seasons in the North Devon countryside. When one thinks of Miss Sutcliff's novels one remembers, as clearly as the details of plot and character, the brilliantly etched details of hills, downs, coastline and villages.

Writing is Rosemary Sutcliff's way of life and it absorbs her completely, so that she is unremitting in the demands she makes on herself. Her work-room is the centre of activity in the house and is guarded by a golden labrador, her constant companion. She begins work in mid-morning and goes on well into the evening with little relaxation, although the telephone and visitors provide constant interruption.

The book begins with about two months of research work after the idea has germinated:

'For me the whole thing starts with the basic idea, which has nothing to do with the plot—that comes later. One basic idea which is, as it were, the seed from which the whole thing grows. It is no good going out to look for this idea. . . . I have to wait and eventually an idea comes, sometimes from outside, from having read something perhaps, or from going to an old house and wondering what the people were like who lived in it when it was new; and sometimes from inside, out of the blue, for no apparent reason at all.'

But if the first awakening of the idea can be called inspiration, what follows is sheer toil.

'I invest in a large red notebook and get to work collecting my notes. I always start off with the encyclopaedia. Not only does it help with a bit of something about everything: it also provides a list of books. So I emerge with a long list of books and then tackle the County Library. Of course, all have bibliographies at the back, and so the thing goes on like a snowball. Little by little . . . the picture begins to emerge.'

Having established and logged the historical background, Miss Sutcliff goes on:

'I get down to what I enjoy much more, re-creating the daily life of the people: the sort of houses they lived in, how they were furnished, what food they ate and how it was cooked, what they grew in their gardens, how they travelled, their clothes and weapons, and, very important from my point of view, what songs they sang and what stories they told round the fire at nights.

'I do not put much of the plot into my red exercise book because it changes so much. . . . I make a draft outline, two or three thousand words, and then start writing. It takes four drafts—or rather three and a fair copy—to get the story properly into shape. That means about eight months' work and usually a couple of months' research beforehand.'

The extent of the research involved in a modern historical novel for children is now always empha-sized, because it was once so easily assumed that they were inaccurate because the truth of fact had to be sacrificed to the demands of plot construction. Although this is no longer a current belief, the actual extent of the background reading may still be underestimated. Rosemary Sutcliff supplied for this monograph a formidable list of the sources for her novel *The Lantern Bearers* which won the Carnegie Medal in 1959.* Yet it is necessary to point out again that exhaustive research into source material could not by itself account for the beauty and artistic integrity of her best novels, which come from the penetrative power of her imagination.

Miss Sutcliff talks of herself and her work with deprecatory humour and good-natured indulgence of the inquirer's curiosity about her method of composition. She writes all her books in longhand, in small clear script. She is not exempt from the demands made on a successful author, and when she is not writing she makes journeys to check details of information or to consult records, answers readers' letters and commentators' queries, and talks to librarians and editors. Miss Sutcliff says that the question she is asked most frequently by reviewers and others is 'How do you *know* about such and such a thing', a detail of social history, topography, seamanship, carefully worked into the texture of the narrative. This gives her most gratification as it means the research material has become part of the organic matter of the story; her painstaking work has been effective. But the secret of Miss Sutcliff's success is more than determination and hard work, although there are plenty of both.

* See appendix on page 71.

Also we should underestimate the achievement and intention of Miss Sutcliff if we assumed that writing stories for children was a compensatory activity. This would fail to account for the distinctive qualities of her art and her personality which can be found only in the novels themselves, and to these we now turn.

II. Childhood and Legend

The urge to tell stories comes directly from having enjoyed them as a child. Most successful storytellers have well-furnished stocks of childhood romances and, as we have seen, Rosemary Sutcliff was no exception. From her earliest attempts she showed her ability to rivet children's attention with a compelling tale.

Her first four books are for younger children: *The Chronicles of Robin Hood* (1950), *The Queen Elizabeth Story* (1950), *The Armourer's House* (1951), and *Brother Dusty-Feet* (1952). They are stories of imaginative fancy set in an historical period which provides the framework, but the fairies and the magic are more important than the kings and queens. Into each story the author reweaves some of the legends which are links with her own childhood delight.

The Chronicles of Robin Hood are retold from the ballads, and the lilt of that strong-limbed verse remains in the prose. There is no attempt to use the familiar outline to construct a work of fiction or to point a moral for the times, as Geoffrey Trease did in *Bows against the Barons* in 1940, when he made Robin Hood a kind of Wat Tyler. Instead, Rosemary Sutcliff keeps the bardic high-seriousness of the legend, filling out the story where description can heighten the plot. The emphasis is on the enchantment of the greenwood and the faithfulness of the sworn band of brothers. There is more idealism than social conscience.

16

The overbearing lords who killed the faithful dog when they seized Robin's farm are the natural victims of the retributive justice which commends this tale to the young of every generation.

'Against the rich merchants and the barons and the pot-bellied churchmen who trample the weak beneath their feet and scoop the possessions of humble folk into their greedy paunches you may do what you will.'

But the outlaws must not harm women, children, or honest poor men. The rules are clear, and mid-twentieth century children can identify the Sheriff of Nottingham and the greedy barons with oppressive adults as others have done before them. Each episode is well-shaped, with the background clearly outlined. The children recognize the word-ritual of the dialogue:

' "With all my heart," cried John. "I will be a loyal man to you all the days of my life." '

The characters are all larger than life, although in the inevitable passion of Robin Hood's death the treacherous Abbess Ursula who is reponsible for it shows signs of greater complexity.

But for all the winter and rough weather, the greenwood is a protective, desirable, sheltered, even cosy place, offering security and escape. It is eminently safe, like the 'den' in children's games, like home. Yet despite its identification with the inner world of the child in his middle period of childhood, *The Chronicles of Robin Hood* shows that Rosemary Sutcliff had, from the outset, the compelling narrative skill of the undoubted storyteller.

· *The Queen Elizabeth Story* is linked with Miss Sutcliff's childhood. It shows her insight into the life of an imaginative little girl accustomed to playing alone. The heroine, Perdita, loves stories, and the one she enjoys best tells how the news came to her Devonshire village of the accession of Queen Elizabeth I. Perdita is a friend of the fairies, so on Midsummer's Eve she asks them to grant her an opportunity to see the great queen before her next birthday. The year goes round with its feasts, fasts and fairs, until the day when the Queen comes on a progress and Perdita sees her. The historical setting of this story is a pageant, a procession of characters in period costume. One's eye is caught from time to time by the beauty of some small detail, the flowers, the weather, the animals. The characters are less convincing. No brother was ever so obliging, no brother's friend ever so attentive to such a little girl. The plot only comes to life when Perdita's brother fights a gypsy for a puppy and when the family is visited by a disturbing great-aunt.

One is tempted to look back on *The Queen Elizabeth Story* with the hindsight that comes from close acquaintance with the later historical novels and to marvel at the author's progress since its appearance. In this early book the heroine is decorative, but puppet-like. The voice of the story-teller is gentle, pleasing but postured. The historical setting is a carefully-worked illuminated edging. The dialogue rarely rises above the commonplaces of social exchange. The narrative power is seen best in the retelling of the legend of *Sir Gawain and the Loathly Lady* and *The Children of Lir*.

These are adult strictures. Children under the age of ten enjoy the book enough to justify a recent reprinting and it gives them a satisfactory introduction to historical novels proper. Signs of the books to come are in the boy hero, Adam Hilyarde, a lame orphan, who, like his creator perhaps, peoples his loneliness with his imagination and brings to life the figures in a tapestry. One can see the author's interest quickening in this more elusive character. He is the first of a line of heroes whose inner life is as significant as their actions. Indeed, despite the over-simplifications, its flower-pretty style and winsomeness, the story has some of the distinctive quality of the later novels.

The feeling of sheltered seclusion persists in both *The Armourer's House* (1951) and *Brother Dusty-Feet* (1952). The first of these was published in the same year as *The Woolpack* by Cynthia Harnett, and although Miss Sutcliff does not attempt the same kind of detailed realism, there is a concern to show the life in the markets and ship-yards and the ways of 'prentices in the London of Henry VIII. The story begins in Devon; Tamsyn is taken from there to live with her armourer uncle, his wife and family. This time the imaginative child shares her play with her cousin Piers, who has secret dreams of going to sea, and together they act out their fantasies of ships and far-off places in the attic where Piers tells Tamsyn tales of voyages to the Indies. The house of the title is warm with fire and candlelight and sweet with herbs and flowers; childhood is idealized. The uncle and aunt are sympathetic and scholarly. The pageant of the year again goes by in the calendar festivals, and neither fever nor unrest mars the comfortable glow. We know at the beginning that the long-lost son will return.

The dialogue still does not match the story-telling; it is uneasily modern. Other authors have shown that to avoid both stilted archaic speech and dated colloquialism a writer of tales with an historical setting must adopt either a form of dateless utterance, and thereby risk a feeling of formality, or else the unashamedly modern, while avoiding slang which soon seems more unreal than the much deplored pishtushery. It was not surprising that reviewers of *The Armourer's House* were unwilling to accept, 'I say, didn't the King's grace look jolly'.

One cannot think of these stories as historical novels. They are a domestication of the past for the younger reader, and this persists even in *Brother Dusty-Feet*, the story of Hugh Copplestone and his dog Argus and how they ran away from wicked Aunt Alison and joined a band of strolling players, who provide for them the charmed circle. Across England they wander and camp at nightfall, their battered costume pack full of the trappings of the heroes in the plays of the legends. This picaresque device for story-telling allows for the inclusion in Hugh's adventures with a strange Palmer, a quack Doctor and a Tom o' Bedlam, but the inset story of Pan and the Stars and the legends of St George and St Aldhelm show once more Miss Sutcliff's skill in narrative and her desire to tell the stories she herself enjoyed. The end of *Brother Dusty-Feet*, when Hugh finds the nobleman to whom his father was sizar at Oxford, is nearly sentimental.

The best episode is 'The Mist Rises'; it has echoes of 'Dimchurch Flit' in *Puck of Pook's Hill* and shows in a characteristic way Miss Sutcliff's debt to Kipling, which she freely acknowledges. Other stories in this Kipling collection were to become of even greater importance later, and we shall have occasion to mention them again.

One might also compare *Brother Dusty-Feet* with Rhoda Power's *Redcap Runs Away*, which has a similar device for the story-telling but is altogether a more substantial book. Miss Power seems to wish to bring the past to life by making stories out of historical material. Miss Sutcliff has a tale to tell for which a historical setting is appropriate; the past comes alive as the result of her involvement in the narrative.

These early books are not to be judged by the standards appropriate to the later ones. They are stories for children written by an author whose skill is developing with each attempt, but who has not yet ventured beyond the fairy-tale in the sheltered world of childhood. The eye for matching details and for the outline of the countryside, the feeling for the passing of the seasons and the weather are at work, but an air of unreality persists throughout the plot, as if there were a lack of passion. When *Simon* appeared in September 1953, those adults who had read Rosemary Sutcliff's earlier books might well have shared the reviewers' surprise at the author's 'sudden and unexpected maturity'. With *Simon* we come to the next stage in Miss Sutcliff's career.

III. The Historical Novelist: (i) *Simon*

Rosemary Sutcliff shares with other writers of historical novels the conviction that 'history matters'. She says: 'Children are prone to grow up seeing history as a series of small static pictures all belonging to Then and having nothing to do with Now.' She sees it as 'a living continuous process of which they themselves are a part'.*

It is not the facts of history that hold the reader of historical novels, but the author's blend of fact and imagination, fired by his enthusiasm. The reader sees himself in real-life situations with the added heroic dimension of time past. His identification with the hero fuses the matter provided by the historian and the imagination supplied by the story-teller.

Since Geoffrey Trease made his plea for better historical fiction for children in *Tales out of School* (1949) and set a consistent standard of artistry for these works, the number of writers who can combine documentary scholarship with narrative skill has increased. Yet Margery Fisher says: 'There are relatively few stories that will swing and startle and electrify a child into real imaginative experience; we must find and hold fast these writers, past and present, who can provide such stories.'†

The clue to the scarcity is in 'real imaginative experience'. On the one hand, the story may bring

---

* Rosemary Sutcliff: *Rudyard Kipling*. Bodley Head Monograph (1960).

† Margery Fisher: *Intent Upon Reading*. Brockhampton (1961).

23

to life a historical period by investing the recorded facts of events with living characters who are not only present on decisive occasions such as battles, but who also eat, sleep, walk over the countryside, pick fights, make friends, feel lost and gradually accumulate experience through which they grow into manhood in the way that every adolescent hopes to do. That historical novels which appeal to adolescents are shot through with idealism is sound psychology. On the other hand, the story may put into a historical setting a universal theme, the nature of friendship, the wastefulness of war and aggression, the consequences of faithfulness, with a hero whose complexity of motive and personality is examined in the light of his time and place. Both kinds of approach involve a high degree of imaginative insight, and although many writers have entered the field of historical novels, sustained excellence is found in comparatively few.

Amongst those who favour the first approach are Ronald Welch, with his dashing, sophisticated tales for boys, and Cynthia Harnett, who among other periods has made familiar the Cotswold wool trade in the fourteenth century and the rich confusion of Caxton's London. In these, details of period are more intricate than motives. History comes alive for the readers of Welch's *Escape from France* when the already familiar events of the Revolution, together with sword fights, escapes and hurried journeys are linked with the distinguished military family of the Careys, who appear in other books in the Crusades, with Marlborough and with

Wellington. When he writes of the fourteenth century in *The Gauntlet*, Welch concentrates on the siege which conveys the feeling and essence of the time. This is vivid history told with gusto. The characters are recognizably modern in speech, yet convincingly of their period.

Authors who are concerned with the universality of history, who see the links of the past with the present as the element they want to present to children, may still write swiftly moving tales with Welch's masculine swing and serve their purpose. Geoffrey Trease is such a writer. In *Bows against the Barons*, Robin Hood, besides being the hero who championed the poor, is described by the author as 'a kind of premature Wat Tyler'. In other novels Trease was anxious to present the allegedly unpopular side of historical situations where history teaching had made children too partisan and therefore slow to understand why men are prepared to die for their beliefs. *Silver Guard* is about the Civil War from the Roundhead viewpoint, and *The Thunder of Valmy* is one of the few books which English children can read to appreciate that the French Revolution involved more than the wrongful imprisonment of aristocrats.

The present popularity of historical novels for children owes much to these authors who were not rebuffed by earlier critics who suggested that 'the future for historical novels is not encouraging',[*]

[*] cf. M. G. Bonner: *The Parent's Guide*. Funk & Wagnall, p. 52 (1926).

and those who agreed with Sir John Marriott that
'the young suspect that there is a maximum of
powder imperfectly concealed in a minimum of
jam'.*

There is also little substantiation for James
Guthrie's criticism which appeared as late as 1958
and finds echoes elsewhere. He says:

'The best contemporary writers for children
retire from the battle† into historical novels. . . .
Patterns can be built up which, so long as they are
internally coherent, need have no close relation to
anything else and children accept historical novels
as a form of higher escapism. . . . It is the lack of
this seriousness, this acknowledgement of the
complexity of living, the universal search for
happiness, the deep unease beneath well-planned
means of getting through the days that makes many
contemporary children's novels ephemeral and
trivial.'‡

This feeling, that historical novels ignored the
real issues, was shared by some conscientious
history teachers, but never by the best writers of
this kind of story for children. They were just as
anxious as Mr Guthrie to acknowledge the complexity of living. No historical novelist can ignore
the brutishness of life in any age. If he does not

* J. A. Marriott: *English History in English Fiction*. Blackie
(1940).
† My italics.
‡ James Guthrie: *Junior Bookshelf* (1958).

26

always choose to dwell on it, he is not necessarily seeking a form of 'higher escapism'.

Rosemary Sutcliff's historical novels show her strong attachment to Kipling. The writing of both authors is shot through with the spirit of the English countryside and the sense of its continuity which links the present with the past. To Kipling, the fact that the Sussex he loved was the same land the Bronze Age villagers knew, the Saxons ploughed and the Normans conquered was to be wondered at. This wonder gives saga, legend and myth modern significance. Miss Sutcliff shares this feeling, and her readers respond to her enthusiasm. Without some communication of feeling for the past the historical novel is lost. When Randal in *Knight's Fee* sits on the hill with the shepherd (the timeless occupation) and handles the flint axe-head which the initiated reader knows was, perhaps, that of Drem in *Warrior Scarlet*, we are made to feel that continuity is important. Kipling finds it entirely significant that the old man who clips the Squire's hedge is descended from one of the same name who clipped the hedge of a knight. This may seem deplorable to progressive egalitarians, but it is one way for children to make the imaginative response that helps the growth of historical awareness.

This sense of place and continuity can be seen in Alison Uttley's *A Traveller in Time* (1939). It is a historical novel with a double time illusion in which the heroine seems to live both in the present and in the past. Although Rosemary Sutcliff has never used this device in a book, one feels that part of her success comes from her ability to do what Miss Uttley demonstrates, to talk 'with people who lived alongside but out of time, moving through a life parallel to my own existence'.* In novels where the time illusion is central, women novelists seem to possess a particular kind of psychological insight, and historical novels written by women show, on the whole, more of the complexity of motive desired by Mr Guthrie.

These elements of continuity in place and time, together with a much greater involvement in a series of historical events, came out strongly in *Simon* (1953), Rosemary Sutcliff's first important historical novel. Miss Sutcliff says of *Simon*:

'It was very much an outside job. It was very nearly written to order. My mother was a great admirer of Oliver Cromwell and she announced one day that she was tired of lovely, lovely Cavaliers, with lovelocks and beautiful manners, and Round-heads with square-toed boots and no manners at all. She wanted a Cavalier and Roundhead story written from the Roundhead point of view for a change.'

These were Geoffrey Trease's feelings when he wrote *The Grey Adventurer* in 1942. The conflicts of this bitter war fire children because they show that men will risk death for their ideals.

Although *Simon* does not deal with the central

* Alison Uttley, Introduction to *A Traveller in Time*. Faber (1939).

issues of the struggle, idealism is the dominant theme. It is a significant book in Miss Sutcliff's development as a writer, for it showed her where her strength lay. It does what she demands history should do, brings to vivid life the actuality of the last campaign of the Civil War which was fought in the combes and across the farmlands of Somerset and North Devon. Miss Sutcliff immersed herself totally in the details and emerged with, for her, a new kind of novel, where pageant is replaced by theme, and all the story-teller's skill is challenged by battles, sieges, troop movements, documentation of personages and events, and the need to account for action in terms of motive as well as circumstance.

Simon is the Roundhead, Amias the Cavalier. Their childhood friendship is wrecked by the war and their conflicting loyalties. No one who had read the early novels would have foreseen that Miss Sutcliff could describe the beating of a deserter, the battle of Torrington and the harsh discomfort of the sick and wounded so evocatively that the waste, pain, misery, glory and excitement of war are held together in a plot compellingly detailed and yet fast-moving. Battles are described in the vivid snatches Simon remembers later:

'Simon heard the strident challenge of the trumpets, and with a roar like a bursting dam, the charge went home. Once again he was sweeping down the street, this time in the wake of Cromwell's leading troop. The Royalists broke back. Lord

Hopton's Blue Coats, caught up in the retreat, were swept away like flotsam on a dark flood. Simon saw their standard waver and go down. He saw Lord Hopton standing in his stirrups as he strove to rally his men, his face white in the moonlight and puddled with blood where a pike had torn his cheek open. Then the mêlée closed between them and he did not see Lord Hopton again.'

When Simon's troop is closing in by night on a country house held by Royalists, the snow and stealth stand out as the abiding memory.

'The windbreak grew thin here, where newly-planted thorn saplings gave poor cover, and it was a case of crawling from now on. On the edge of the home paddock they came upon another sentry post, and here the guard were on the alert and there was a scuffle and the beginning of a cry followed by the crack of a musket stock on somebody's head; then a long prickling silence in which the men, crouching in the black gloom of the paddock trees, waited with straining ears for any sound of an alarm. None came.'

Many an author has described a battle with exactness, but Miss Sutcliff's method of settling on the felt details that remain in the mind, driven along the nerves of the hero, is even more convincing than the historian's account. The intensity of the inner life of the author, at which the earlier books hinted, has been projected into the teeming outside world of the Civil War. Her sympathies

are shared, but her bias is towards the Roundheads.
To grasp the quality and personal involvement, one
can compare *Simon* with Trease's *The Grey
Adventurer* which is equally skilful but much more
detached. Sometimes Miss Sutcliff is carried away
by the pressure of detail, but the line of action is
held taut throughout the book. All round her as
she wrote it she saw the hills and fields of North
Devon over which her heroes had ridden. The
detailed outline of field, farm and hiding place are
as clearly visualized as the organization of the
battles.

In *Simon* Miss Sutcliff leaves the sheltered world
of childhood and enters the realm where public
excellence is tested and recognized. Her heroes
are separated by differing sympathies in the war,
but they are true to what they believe, so that their
friendship is sealed at the very moment they fight
each other. The theme is for a reader older than
any Miss Sutcliff had in mind before this. Loyalty
and devotion, the conflicts and complexities of
war, are beyond the immediate grasp of the under-
tens but within the compass of the twelve-year-old
who is beginning to recognize these very conflicts
in his own terms. Both author and reader are
identified with the hero's development, and both
have grown in stature as a result.

As this happens, the conscious narrative tone of
the earlier books falls away. A greater breadth of
vocabulary and longer sentences are possible. With
Simon, Rosemary Sutcliff becomes a writer for the
child who is a discriminating reader, one who asks

that his books should extend his experience and stretch his ability to the full.

Not only is *Simon* longer, more complex, and more strongly felt than the earlier books, it also shows a new depth of characterization and a totally unexpected skill in dialogue based on the rhythms of local Devonshire speech. Simon's corporal, Zeal-for-the-Lord Relf, whose desire for private vengeance is used as a counterpoise to the theme of loyalty in the main plot, is a fine study in excessive fervour. Pentecost Fiddler is the itinerant Palmer of *Brother Dusty-Feet*, but with a significant local function and local speech. Colonel Fairfax is sternly heroic and Cromwell suitably shadowy. With new vigour and conviction Rosemary Sutcliff moved away from the tempting delight of historical tales for the younger reader and the threat of escapism. Now real history, the kind that demands not only passion and zeal in the telling but also painstaking checking of detail and careful assimilation of the spirit of an age, had superseded the lure of legend. Looking back, one can see *Simon* as a turning point in Rosemary Sutcliff's career. It has all the seeds of promise that flowered later. Interestingly, the hero is robust and finely-balanced within himself from the start. He has depths of sense and sensibility unusual in adventure story heroes; he suffers anguish from his divided loyalties, but keeps faith above all, and comes through by virtue of a sound constitution and an even temper. None of the heroes who follow begin with these advantages.

IV. The Historical Novelist: (ii) The Light and the Dark

One of the benefits of a classical education in days gone by was a working familiarity with life in ancient Rome. Sometimes one wonders what Dr Johnson would say about the modern schoolboy's ignorance of Pliny and Horace and his familiarity with the towns, villas and heating systems of Roman Britain. In the last decade, novelists have made the young free of the camps and fortifications the legions built, especially the settlements in the south and along Hadrian's wall, so that one finds in a succession of children's books the same streets, wineshops, cooking facilities, military arrangements, threatening Picts, Saturnalia, and baths. The writers have evoked all the hustle of effective colonization and military conquest with enough skill to revive the drooping fortunes of Latin and to bring to life the period between the leap into the sea of Caesar's standard-bearer and the sailing away of the last Roman galley.

The interest provided by the details is linked to the adventure of a hero, as in Henry Treece's *Legions of the Eagle*, which deals with the friendship of the son of a Belgic chieftain with a Roman soldier. It is interesting to compare tales dealing with this period, as the same sources are used while the methods differ greatly. *Word to Caesar* (Geoffrey Trease), *They Fought for Brigantia* (Marjorie Rowling), *The Mistletoe and the Sword* (Anya Seton) show the variety of the authors' skill and approach, while *The Eagles have Flown* (Henry Treece), *The Last of Britain* and *Merlin's King* (Meriol Trevor) indicate the attraction of the twilight period when the Romans were evacuating Britain. On the whole the emphasis is on action, the narration of incident, a mission accomplished, a march, a battle, although the desire to recreate the Roman *virtus* is also prevalent. Not unnaturally it bears a recognizable resemblance to the sportsmanship of our own day.

An exceptional book in this category is Stephanie Plowman's *To Spare the Conquered* (1960) which depicts Rome as an occupying power in Britain, troubled with the responsibilities the conqueror has for the victims. The hero, Quintus, and others see the mission of Rome as an exercise in preserving the dignity of man at a time when Rome itself was losing imperial stature and the colonies were being exploited to maintain the crumbling façade. The story covers the rising of the Iceni ruler, Boudicca, and gives the author scope to examine the motives of the Roman commanders, centurions and procurators. It is a book worth comparing with those of Miss Sutcliff on this period, as both writers are concerned with the mainsprings of action and the temperamental differences of personality, as well as the thronging life of the legions.

Rosemary Sutcliff has written four books which deal with this period: *The Eagle of the Ninth* (1954), *The Silver Branch* (1957), *The Lantern Bearers* (1959) and *Outcast* (1955). The first three form a sequence in that they deal with the fortunes of the family of Marcus Flavius Aquila, the centurion who came to Britain in the hope of finding what happened to his father's legion, the legendary Ninth, when it marched beyond the Wall and was never heard of again. *Outcast* is about the life of a slave in the galleys which brought the legions to Britain. *Dawn Wind* (1961) is the chronological sequel to *The Lantern Bearers*. It links the books of the first Roman period with the coming of the Christian missionaries to Kent.

These books enjoy widespread popularity both here and abroad and have contributed most to Miss Sutcliff's reputation. *The Eagle of the Ninth* has been reprinted four times, broadcast twice in its entirety, and has even found its way into a textbook in which it is used as a model for writing for children.* The imaginative scope and power of these books were barely hinted at before *Simon*, and the artistic maturity of *The Lantern Bearers* scarcely even glimpsed. Reviewers, detecting the Kiplingesque overtones, have accused or praised the heroes according to their prejudices about Kipling ('young Britons at outposts of Empire rather than young Romans on the Wall'), but they have freely admitted that the books make challenging reading for adults as well as children.† The thematic material repays close study if one is concerned to know the author as an artist and a personality, and from the outset we cannot fail to be persuaded that here

* *Creative Writing in English.* Gordon Taylor. Allen and Unwin (1960).

† *The Eagle of the Ninth* is in both children's and adults' sections of many public libraries.

is a body of work which satisfies, without modification or concession, the claim that this writer for children is an artist in her own right.

The root of the matter is no secret, yet it defies exact interpretation beyond saying that the vital spark of Rosemary Sutcliff's books, from *The Eagle of the Ninth* onwards, is the total imaginative penetration of the historical material. The books seem to be written from the inside, so that the reader's identification with the chief character carries him further into the *felt* life of the time than many other books which are made up of the skilful but detached articulation of the fruits of research. One feels that Rosemary Sutcliff is less concerned to write historical narrative than to reconstruct, in the child's response to her creative imagination, a strong feeling for and involvement with the people of this mist-bound, huddling, winter-dark island at the periods when the invaders came, Romans, Saxons, Norsemen.

This magic has certain recognizable elements; the names of the characters are chosen with a poet's care, the dogs have a central place and are characterized with the loving attention children recognize and approve. The villains, such as Placidus in *The Eagle of the Ninth* and Allectus in *The Silver Branch* are acidly etched, although there is more reliance on traditional enmity and feud than on personal evil to provide the dark side. Episodic characters, singly or in groups, have a miniaturist's clarity of outline. Pandarus, the gladiator with his rose in the battle, Galerius the surgeon, the garrulous household slaves, soldiers at a firelit cockfight or warriors at a feast, all are equally memorable. Others more involved in the developing action, commanding officers, wise men of the tribes, outcasts, especially Guern the Hunter, Evicatos of the Spear and Brother Ninnias, have a legendary quality. Tradui the Chieftain at the making of New Spears, Bruni, dressed in the war gear of a Jutish hero dying as the wild geese fly south, blind Flavian, killed at the hands of marauding Saxons, all carry a dignity and heroism that link this series of tales with the legends Miss Sutcliff loves to tell. Indeed, part of the difficulty in evaluating the achievement of these books comes from the thickly woven texture which is as closely wrought as in many adult novels of quality.

Now that the standard of accredited detail is so high in historical novels, writers have their research material carefully scrutinized by critics. It is one thing to be accurate about costume and cooking pots, and quite another to make an organic whole in which the accumulated research is assimilated by the reader because of its essential *rightness* in the situation. Here is Wroxeter when the Romans had left it and later the British warhost had finally been defeated.

'Owain found himself at the Forum Gate, with its proud inscription to the Emperor Hadrian, and halted there, staring dazedly about him, while Dog stood watching him expectantly and wagging his tail. It was growing dusk, and he thought suddenly

37

—it was a thought that made the sick laughter rise in his throat—that he could sleep in the Basilica tonight, he could sleep in the Palace of Kyndylan the Fair, if he chose, he was free of all Viroconium. But the little low-browed shops in the Forum colonnade seemed to offer a deeper and darker refuge to crawl into. One or two near the gate still had their roofs on them and he turned into the nearest of these. It looked to have been a basket-maker's shop; everything that could be of use to marauders had been stripped from it, but a broken pigeon basket and a bunch of withies still lay in one corner. The light was going fast, and the back of the shop was already lost in the shadows of the rainy twilight.'*

Weather and the ruined town all serve to increase Owain's desolation. The scholarship is transmuted into artistry.

Each plot is full of incident and suspense, the construction is taut but supple. Each book has a unified theme, yet they are linked together. In *The Eagle of the Ninth*, Marcus Flavius Aquila is invalided out of his legion after his first battle in Britain. When his wound has healed, he goes with his freed slave, Esca, to look for the eagle of the lost Ninth Legion and to learn his father's fate. *The Silver Branch* tells how the torn eagle, many years later, goes into battle again at the head of a ragged band of men loyal to Rome at a time when her power is being undermined by rival emperors

* *Dawn Wind*, p. 29.

and Britain is being invaded by Saxon war bands. The heroes are Justin and Flavius, descendants of the first Marcus, whose farm, which is now Flavius's, serves as a meeting place for men secretly in the service of Rome. The arrival of Constantius establishes the Roman peace once more, although we feel it cannot be for long. *The Lantern Bearers* deals with the period when the Romans have left Britain to the warring Hengist and Vortigern and the young Roman-British Ambrosius. Aquila, racked with bitterness against the Saxons for his father's murder, his sister's disappearance and his own thralldom in Jutland, spends years of hardship fighting the Saxons before he learns to be at peace within himself. *Dawn Wind* begins with the last defeat of the Britons by the Saxons at Aquae Sulis, and covers the twelve years that follow. The British hero, Owain, becomes the thrall of a Saxon farmer and his case seems even more hopeless than Aquila's, until the Welsh envoy at the court of the Saxon king tells him that there is a 'dawn wind stirring' in the arrival of the Roman monk, Augustine, at Canterbury.

In narrative, *The Eagle of the Ninth* is the most workmanlike; each incident has a bold outline, fire-clear details, and is told with passion and skill. The others cover larger stretches of time and the canvas is more crowded. As the subtlety of plot and theme grows more complex, so the author looks to older readers. The publishers say that the expected age-range is eleven to sixteen, which is, roughly, the main period of adolescence, and part of the author's success lies in the skill with which she interprets the complex emotional responses of this phase of her readers' development.

The theme of each book is the light and the dark. The light is what is valued, what is to be saved beyond one's own lifetime. The dark is the threatening destruction that works against it. The heroes are serious young men schooled in the Roman virtues of *pietas* and *gravitas* which demand loyalty to family, country, friend and cause, exactly those things which call out the idealism of adolescents whose inner world is full of this kind of thinking. Marcus goes to look for his father's eagle as an act of piety and also that he may compensate for the loss of his own command. In so doing, he learns other loyalties, to the land of Britain as well as to Rome, to his slave who becomes his friend, and about the nature of loyalty itself, how it grew hollow in the lost legion, how men mistake the true for the false, that honour must be paid for many times, that freedom is not simply manumission. To become adult is to learn these things in different ways. As in *Simon*, public excellence is seen as the extension of private virtues. It is recognized by men of all tribes, by those who move in the darkness beyond the Wall as well as by those to whom duty is the clear call of a military trumpet. This is what the young want to know about in an age when they are faced by equivocal adult standards and general cynicism.

This theme is extended in *The Silver Branch* with increased subtlety, for the creativeness of the

Roman peace is now threatened by the wanton destructiveness of the Saxons and the darkness at the heart of those who threaten the order that Rome brought to the barbarians. Justin and Flavius are impelled by Carausius's words to risk all for him, even after he is dead:

' "If I can make this one province strong—strong enough to stand alone when Rome goes down, then something may be saved from the darkness. If not, then Dubris light and Limanis light and Rutupiae light will go out. The lights will go out everywhere." He stepped back, dragging aside the hanging folds of the curtain, and stood framed in their darkness against the firelight and lamplight behind him, his head yet turned to the grey and silver of the starry night.'

The chances of saving the light are no stronger than the little silver branch carried by the Emperor's fool, 'shining drops distilled out of the emptiness'. This may be a partial view of the Pax Romana, but it speaks to the young who are constantly reminded of past glories when these are now so obviously lacking, and who have no firm assurance that their world will emerge from the darkness that threatens it.

The Lantern Bearers is the most closely-woven novel of the trilogy. The committee of the Carnegie Award did well to wait for the third volume before honouring Miss Sutcliff. In it the hero bears within himself the conflict of dark and light, the

burden of his time and of himself. When he fires
the beacon of Rutupiae light for the last time 'as a
defiance against the dark' and goes wilful-missing
to stay in Britain, to which he feels he belongs,
Aquila is carrying the Roman *virtus* into the next
age. At the end of the book he says, 'I wonder if
they will remember us at all, these people on the
other side of the darkness'. To this theme there is a
rich counterpoint of personality and event, motive
and action, more intricately interwoven than in any
novel so far.

After his thralldom with the Jutes, Aquila's
darkness is at his heart, for loyalties betrayed and
vengeance sought. All gentleness is shut out. At
moments of the greatest turbulence when the darkness is closing round, Aquila realizes that the light
men carry within them, which is the only safeguard
against the greater darkness of despair, is their
concern for each other and what is dear to them.
Gradually from his wife, Ness, and Brother
Ninnias, Aquila learns that love and loyalty are
more than the quickly-lost ideals of youth. A man
may serve a cause so that his public excellence can
be recognized, and yet one who remains untouched
by family love and warmth for others is still in
darkness, for all his *virtus*. The glory that was
Rome is no longer; all that remains is an ideal in
the hearts of men who have risen above common
vengeance, and the races must learn to be at peace
together.

This theme is continued in *Dawn Wind*. Owain
has more than served his time as a thrall, yet he does

not leave the family he has lived with because he made a promise to his master that was more binding than his thrall ring. Einon Hen, the Welsh envoy, explains to Owain his vision of the light and the dark since the departure of the Romans and during the between-time that followed:

'Owain, hasn't it ever seemed to you that a strange thing is happening between the British and the Saxon kind? It is three generations since Artos died, and the years between have been lost and dark and very bloody, so that if one looks backward it is as though one peered through the night and storm to catch the last brave glimmer of a lantern very far behind . . . Now this Beornwulf turns to you, a Briton, in his last and sorest need of a friend, and for four years of your life, and maybe more to come, you have shouldered the weight of a Saxon household, and you sit there and ask me . . . "What else could I do?"—And that, do you know, is a thing that I find more filled with promise than any treaty between Aethelbert and the Princess of the Cymru. Almost it is as though, looking forward this time, one might perhaps make out another gleam of light very far ahead.'

This intricacy of theme is kept jewel-clear in all the books by an adept handling of symbolic material, a ritualism which young readers appreciate. It is full of surcharged emotion which need not be uttered: Marcus setting up his little altar to Mithras and sacrificing the bird of carved olive

43

wood, symbolizing his childhood and former life, the Dolphin ring which links the family through the ages, the fish symbol drawn in the ashes of the hearth by the legionary, the tattooed dolphin on Aquila's shoulder, the recurrent symbolism of flowers, herbs, colours, and the ritual return of seasons, blossom and fruit, sowing and sacrifice.

Remembering the gentle cosiness of Miss Sutcliff's early books, one might be surprised to find the uncompromising cruelty of the battles portrayed with equally uncompromising clarity. The white heat of Aquila's controlled emotion in *The Lantern Bearers*, its total rejection of comfort and gentleness, has no precedent in her work. Treachery, hardship, the ferocity of friend and foe are set down with an intensity of imaginative passion, as if the author were concerned to prove the lasting qualities of the virtues that are tried in the fire of conflict.

The darkness of *The Eagle of the Ninth* is of a particular quality, the magic and the ritual of the primitive tribes, which Miss Sutcliff conveys with distinctive success. These are monumental powers evoking primeval impulses:

'A figure stooped out under the low lintel into the torchlight. The figure of a man, stark naked save for the skin of a grey dog-seal, the head drawn over his own. The Seal Clan greeted his coming with a quick rhythmic cry that rose and fell and rose again, setting the blood jumping back to the heart. For an instant the man—Seal-priest or man-seal—stood before them, receiving their acclamation, then with the clumsy shuffling motion of a seal on dry land, moved to one side of the doorway; and another figure sprang out of the darkness, hooded with the snarling head of a wolf. One after another they came, naked as the first had been, their bodies daubed with strange designs in woad and madder, their head-dresses of animal pelts or bird-feathers, the wings of a swan, the pelt of an otter with the tail swinging behind the wearer's back, the striped hide of a badger shining black and white in the torchlight.'

Adults may admire the skill with which the chapter 'The Feast of the New Spears' is written. Young readers respond to the excitement of the ceremonial darkness and fiery torchlight because they can feel rather than discuss its significance. When the early books put feelings into words they were lost in sentimentality. Here the emotion is all the stronger for the symbolical representation. This book, by its combination of swift narrative and varied episodes, remains the readers' favourite as it is the author's.

When we examine these particular instances of Miss Sutcliff's craft we see that the effectiveness of the whole, which moves with the speed and sweep of the narrative to the climax of each episode, is nevertheless composed of minute attention to detail: the colour of the sky, the shape of the hills, the mane of a horse, a bowl of apples or words carved on a rock, all are invested with meaning.

In these Roman stories the problem of dialogue

has been solved by the invention of timeless cadences in a slightly shifted word order, the surest safeguard against stilted archaism or colloquialism, even though the fall of the phrase is sometimes unreal, or occasionally the modern speaker peeps out. Also the girls, who were not so well-drawn as the boys, have gradually assumed more weight. Ness, Aquila's wife, is a character of quality, whereas Cottia, Marcus's friend, is altogether too babyish. As her characters mature, so does the author's handling of dialogue.

In between the books of the trilogy are three others: *Outcast* (1955), *The Shield Ring* (1956) and *Warrior Scarlet* (1958) and a short story of life on the Roman Wall, *The Bridge Builders*, which although published in 1959 seems from the author's note to have been written before *The Shield Ring* was completed. Although Miss Sutcliff has developed into a story-teller who is at her best in a long narrative, this short sketch has her unmistakable individuality.

Outcast, the story of Beric, can be mentioned here as it has a link with the others discussed in this chapter, and it throws light on an important aspect of the novels. Beric is washed up on the shores of Britain and adopted by a tribe which later casts him out. He is carried off to Rome as a slave. In making a bid for freedom he is recaptured and sent to the galleys where, after unspeakable treatment, he attacks an overseer, is lashed and dropped into the sea for dead. The sea casts him up again, this time on Romney Marsh where he falls into the hands of Justinius, the 'Builder of Roads and Drainer of Marshes', who adopts him as his son. Together they fight the great gale that threatens the dyke and the work to which Justinius's life is dedicated.

This is another fast-moving story, yet the plot depends to a greater extent than usual on coincidence, legitimate as this is, and is more loosely episodic. The two outstanding features are the descriptive reality of the life of a galley slave and the dark misery of the outcast, which anticipates Aquila's torments in *The Lantern Bearers*. Beric belongs nowhere; he has no tribe, his Roman master give him another name, a galley slave has no identity. Finally Justinius seems to have mistaken him for someone else, the son he had never seen.

To the adolescent the theme of 'Who am I?' is a compelling one. In his desire to be accepted for the person he is, to establish his identity in the adult world, to find a role he can play, he identifies himself with the outcast, a part which, for all its misery, he fully understands. The characterization of Beric might well have fallen into sentimentality, but this is avoided. It is debatable, however, whether it avoids altogether an excess of self-laceration that is more than the realistic cruelty conventional in the Roman tales of other writers, notably those of Henry Treece. Adult reviewers have objected to the scenes of lashings, while young people have told Miss Sutcliff that they enjoyed them. They are neither excessive nor distasteful, but they hint at something deeper in the plight of the hero, which the other three Roman books also illustrate.

After his first battle Marcus, in *The Eagle of the Ninth*, endures rough-and-ready doctoring and later penetrating surgery to search his wounds which leave him with a limp and exclude him from regular military service. He undertakes his special mission with a handicap. Justin, in *The Silver Branch* is a disappointment to his father as he is a surgeon, not a fighting man. He stutters and lacks self-assurance in his dealings with people. Aquila, in *The Lantern Bearers*, has withdrawn from close human relationships and is something of a maimed personality. The scar on his brow is the merest outward sign of his inward scars. Beric distrusts all kindness as the result of the treatment he has undergone:

'There was no place for him there, after all, no place for him anywhere in the world of men that had cast him out, and made him a slave and sent him to the galleys. He would go to the wild and be done with men!'

Only in their relationship with others, the ideal companion, the blood brother, the wise man, do these wounds heal. The cautery is sharp and stinging. Marcus must submit to searching knives in his leg and also to finding out the bitter truth about the Ninth Legion. He learns too from Esca the uneasy relations between slave and freeman when these are complicated by pride. Justin has to learn to forget himself, to lose himself in the cause where arms are useless weapons until the end. Aquila keeps his inner darkness as a kind of protection so that he need not be touched by feeling; he recovers when he lets emotion in again.

One feels in reading these books that the inner life of the hero is as important as any outward action. The heroic man is of a certain cast of temper, a mould, a balance, which is no more and no less than we learn in the *Iliad* and the tales of Arthur. The conflict of the light and the dark is the stuff of legend in all ages. Miss Sutcliff's artistry is a blend of this realization in her own terms and an instructive personal identification with problems which beset the young, problems of identity, of self-realization. Children see in stories of maimed and hurt children struggles with conscience rather than with the outside world. Extended into adolescence these struggles increase in intensity. The young respond with imaginative sympathy to those who are in any way handicapped and they do not shy away from the didacticism or moralizing implicit in these figures. As the heroes come to see that one must learn to carry one's scars lightly by acceptance and concern for others, so do the readers.

Being an outcast may mean that one feels rejected, different, but it is also an attitude of mind by which one takes revenge on others. One is less of a person if one is preoccupied with one's own hurts. Only by being involved in something creative, the search for the Eagle, the maintenance of law in a disordered world, the building of a wall against the sea, the farming of the land, does one find oneself.

In *Dawn Wind* one sees that internal battles in England solve fewer and fewer problems. The different tribes and races must learn to live with each other. The last conquest is still to come, but the lesson holds good.

v. The Central Theme

The pace-makers in any art form are those who dispel our preconceptions about the form itself. Compared with them are books written for children by hundreds of painstaking and conscientious craftsmen who apply the formulae which have proved efficient. Many succeed in infusing much new life into well-worn skeletons. But the outstanding books dare to step outside the conventions which decree whether a story is too 'involved' or 'difficult' for the young and provide them with a distinctive imaginative viewpoint from which they see themselves afresh. Adults demand this as a matter of course. Lately it has been clear that older children do the same.

We have seen that Rosemary Sutcliff can not only revivify the twilight period between the age of Imperial Rome and the coming of Christianity, but also create heroes whose standards of values reflect her readers' awareness of the conflict between private conduct and public excellence in a way that extends beyond the limits of formula fiction. In another three books, *The Shield Ring*, *Warrior Scarlet* and *Knight's Fee*, written in between the Roman stories, Miss Sutcliff tackles the most pressing problem of all: how does one win one's place in the world of men? What are the conditions of acceptance? To a writer like Miss Sutcliff, whose circumstances as a child cut her off from much that other children could take for granted, this question had a special significance.

Miss Sutcliff is fully identified with everything she writes, and we have traced her development as a writer in the growing complexity of the themes she has chosen. The books of this chapter highlight three specific 'traces' of importance to an understanding of her work and her personality. They concern the permanence of landscape, which is the Kipling tradition; the settling in England of races or peoples who learn to live together so that their original identity is blended in a new nationality, and the *rite de passage* from youth to manhood, which is, I feel, the central theme.

All three traces are present in *The Shield Ring*, the story about Norsemen who withstood the entry of King William's Norman troops into the Lake District at the making of the Domesday Book. The tribal valour and clan loyalty of the Norsemen formed a 'shield ring' and the Normans were lured up a specially made road that led to nowhere and slaughtered in ambush. From a study of place names and local legend, the author has recreated Lakeland as it was in Jarl Buthar's day, not only as a scholar, but as an artist whose eye can select the details, which, combined with intensity of narration, bring alive the fells, lakes and rock ledges as the tale unfolds, especially in the high and empty places:

'The fellside dropped away from her with a rush and a falcon swoop that almost took her breath away. Far, far below her lay the green ribbon of Rannardale with its thread of a brook winding between steep woods of birch and hazel, down to the Crumbeck Water. Down there at the head of the Dale she could make out the ancient steading of that Ragna who had given his name to the place in the early days of the Northmen's coming, part roofless now, and long since sunk to be a shepherd's boothe, and the little pattern of old fields, once deserted, that had come into their own again since the Jarl made his Shield Ring in Butharsdale.'

It is difficult for critics to believe that Miss Sutcliff has never visited the Lakes.

The landscape in *Warrior Scarlet* is the Sussex Downs, those same hills that Kipling found so full of historical significance. *Warrior Scarlet* is set in the Bronze Age, the age of the heroic Golden People. But long before their time an unknown ancient warrior slept under the Hill of Gathering, the Bramble Hill of *Knight's Fee*, which deals with the Sussex Downs when Senlac fight was a living memory. The Little Dark People who lived there before the Golden People came are still there in the Conqueror's day in the shepherd and the wise woman. So the earth remains. This spell of continuity, Miss Sutcliff's best legacy from Kipling, is woven long and wide in a way that Kipling no more than hinted at. The plots of Miss Sutcliff's three stories are bound fast to the soil. The Norsemen know that they will gradually blend with the people round about; the Normans learn that they must settle disputes in accordance with customs now long established. This feeling for the continuing survival of the land is the true historical sense of Miss Sutcliff's novels. Where other novelists for children have portrayed this sense of continuity they have been involved in the chronicle aspects of their material, the unwinding of a tale of successive generations, as in a novel like *The Land the Ravens Found*, by Naomi Mitchison, so that although we could retrace the steps of the families which moved from Caithness to Iceland, so vivid and exact are the details, we miss the mounting tension of *The Shield Ring* which concentrates on a single climax. In it there is the deep brooding fear of being hunted that haunts each episode, a feeling that only by supreme efforts, by surpassing themselves, will the Norsmen survive. The countryside takes on the significance of a human character, especially at night or in time of battle. It is never simply a setting.

The Shield Ring begins with Frytha, driven from her home as a child when the Normans set fire to it and carried into Lakeland by a faithful shepherd. But the central conflict concerns Bjorn, the orphan who grows up to be a warrior and a harper. Frytha alone knows the question with which Bjorn torments himself. What would he do if he were captured and tortured by the enemy? Would he tell them what they wanted to know? Would he break under torture and become like the mazelin, the half-creature whom they found in the hills? To prove himself, Bjorn knows when the time comes that he must go as a minstrel into the Norman camp to bring back details of their strength. The only way to rid himself of his fear and to be a man is to face what he dreads. The taunt of cowardice which has hung over him since childhood cannot be gainsaid in any other way. The climax of the book comes when Bjorn gives proof of his courage—at a price—before the final battle begins.

A reviewer remarked that Miss Sutcliff 'will always put down her harp for a battle'. We have seen that it was not so in the early books, but after *The Eagle of the Ninth* she has made contact with the mainsprings of feeling in her adolescent readers. It is important for them that Bjorn should not fail, for they share his secret fears about the testing day, his driving need to be found worthy. It is a theme common to other books, but in few others is the author so identified with the hero in the day of trial. For all that crises come to the young in other guises nowadays, the conflict is no less. Miss Sutcliff's resolution is, fear is to be faced, not fled from, lest manhood and self-respect be lost for ever.

In *Knight's Fee*, Randal, the dog-boy of Arundel Castle, is won by a Norman minstrel in a chess game and handed over to Sir Everard d'Aiguillon to be a valet and companion for his grandson, Bevis. Randal has been ill-treated all his childhood and learns the mutuality of friendship with difficulty, although he has the faithfulness of the hounds he loves because they have been his brothers. Randal proves himself, becomes Bevis's squire and fights with him at Tenchebrai, another exciting battle climax. There had never been any possibility of knighthood for Randal as he had neither money nor land with which to furnish his helm. Bevis, dying on the battlefield, gives Randal his accolade, and he gains his manor by keeping faith with the minstrel who first won him from the Lord of Arundel.

The theme is again that of Marcus and Esca, set this time in the uneasy beginning of the Norman period. The allegiances of vassal and lord and the knightly code are seen to involve more than the exacted duties of the feudal system. Indeed, the classroom details of manorial holdings are transformed into real situations so that one scarcely notices the didacticism. Randal's chief difficulty is not lack of status but his inability to believe that people will use him well, which makes him feel that he is always on the edge of his group, not wholly accepted if not quite an outcast. This gives *Knight's Fee* a certain tragic grimness. Not that it lacks gaiety; there is a most spirited heroine. But the emphasis is on the loneliness of the knightly vigil, and here, as in no earlier book, the ideal companion, the sworn brother, dies, so that the central figure emerges into full stature alone. Randal's loneliness is a vigil of another kind; it consists of keeping faith with the minstrel, with the villainous knight who coveted the manor, and above all with the manor itself when Bevis is dead.

This book breaks new ground in dealing with the Norman period and the problem of resolving the differences of those who have to live side by side in England. Miss Sutcliff has no preference for

Norman or Saxon; she cares for the land and its people. *Knight's Fee* is a book of sound workmanship. Although it lacks the driving intensity of *The Lantern Bearers* and *Warrior Scarlet*, it has a new detachment, as if the author were watching her own skill at work with a certain confidence.

It is well for a critic to confess a preference. *Warrior Scarlet* has been kept until last because I am persuaded that it shows Rosemary Sutcliff's art at its best and combines the qualities of the other tales with a controlled intensity of writing which produces a work of great power and authenticity. Also, I feel that in this book author and reader are most truly identified. For the reader the theme is the one which most concerns the adolescent, that of becoming adult. For the writer the problem is to vivify a period beyond written record, to write a book about the heroic age as compelling as legend itself.

Because we no longer have any recognizable ceremony of initiation, adolescents begin to demand recognition as adults as soon as they can adopt adult roles. Society complicates matters by allowing them to drive a car, enlist in the army, marry, vote, all at different ages, and the certainty of having gained adult status seems elusive. They are also expected to act responsibly before they are given responsibility. In *Warrior Scarlet* the reader sees the problem in clear outline against the background of a heroic age where the demands of the tribe are

57

unequivocal: after a wolf is slain in single combat, the boy hunts with the Men's Side. What if he fails? He is no longer of the Golden People. He is an outcast and keeps sheep with the Little Dark People whom the golden warriors once dispossessed of their lands and to whom tribal privileges no longer extend.

In *Warrior Scarlet* Rosemary Sutcliff has widened her range to cover the hinterland of history and realized, with the clarity we have come to expect, every aspect of the people of the Bronze Age, from hunting spears and cooking pots to king-making and burial customs, from childhood to old age. The book is coloured throughout with sunset bronze. The chief episodes are at dusk: the arrival of the smith with the first iron dagger, the hound fight in the glow of the night fire at the king-making, the final wolf-slaying in the red winter twilight.

'And so, while the flame of the sunset blazed and sank behind the Hill of Gathering, as though the sacred fires blazed there as they did at Beltane, and the faint smell of frost and dead leaves stole up from the forest to mingle with the sharp, blue reek of wood smoke and horse droppings, the bronze-smith brought forth his treasures, laying them first before the Chieftain, then passing them among the eager hands of tribesmen: beautifully shaped axe-heads, spear blades all of bronze, neck rings and arm rings of shining bronze and silver and copper, ornaments for a pony's harness, and a sword with studs of red coral on the unguarded hilt. There was little bargaining as yet, men looked at the things they wanted, making no comment; and in a little they would go home and think about it, and see what they had to give in exchange, and come back in the morning maybe with a length of cloth or a couple of fine beaver skins or a lathe-turned beechen bowl.'

The important episodes are linked with the scarlet cloth that is woven for a boy who becomes a man after his wolf-slaying, and the story is of Drem, whose right arm is withered and for whom the world changed on the day when he came home without being seen and heard his Grandfather ask:

'Is it likely, think you, that the young one will win his way into the Men's Side with a spear arm he cannot use?'

Thereafter everything seems to urge home the fact that he will never be a man; his brother's hint that he will never wield a bow, an overturned bowl of stew. Drem, lashing himself into a fury of anger 'as a shield against fear', rushes into the woods where he is found by Talore, the great one-armed hunter to whom he confides his secret fear. Talore says that on the day he is presented to the tribe after his wolf-slaying he will stand with him. More than that, he lets Drem have Whitethroat, one of the best of his wolfhound cubs, in return for his first kill with a throw-spear.

From then on Drem concentrates with ferocious
intensity on the trial to come. He fights for, and
wins, his place in the Boys' House and gains the
friendship of the chieftain's son. He fights in single
combat at the king-making and proves himself
worthy before his time. In fact, he tries too hard,
is too intensely self-absorbed, and despite his
preparation and skill he misses his wolf and seems
to be for ever excluded from the tribe. He must go
to Doli and the sheep. With pain and anguish he
learns the deep simple wisdom of the shepherds,
humility, self-knowledge and patience which are
the only cure for *hubris*, and his pent-up anger
gradually abates. The climax comes when Drem
saves Doli and a ewe from the wolves and meets
his own wolf again, this time to kill him and to
win his Warrior Scarlet.

No summary of the plot can do justice to the
power and sweep of this tale and the depth of the
relationships portrayed. Doli and the shepherd kind
are as heroic after their fashion as the chieftain's
spearbearers, and the virtues they teach are
courage, tenacity, care for simple things and
patience. Drem learns with difficulty. He does not
realize that Blai, the pale girl left behind at his
hearth, is an outcast too. He does not see that she
championed him and expected nothing in return,
and he rejects her fellowship when he most needs it
because she has seen him humiliated when he
gave vent to his temper on the sheep and was rude
to the shepherds. He cannot believe that Votrix, his
blood brother, shared his panic and shame, so he is

surly with him. The restrained dialogue in the scene when they meet after Drem's disgrace is masterly. Only gradually Drem learns not to take revenge on the world for the arm he cannot use, until at the last he proves himself, as do the other maimed heroes, by forgetting himself.

Drem's coming to manhood is more than his growing skill to conquer his disability. He sees the power and beauty of the swan he killed.

'Desolation as piercing as the moment of vision had been stabbed through him. How could a little spear that he had thrown almost without knowing it, blot out in an instant all the power and the swiftness and the shining?'

He learns to see sheep as a shepherd sees them and to put his own concerns aside while looking after them. He comes to realize that although his world had been 'a harsh one in which the pack turned on the weakest hound, in which little mercy was asked or given', the real achievement is to face the fear, to carry the disability, to save one's life by risking it entirely.

Miss Sutcliff shows again her great artistry in dealing with the menace of dark rituals. The making of New Spears, a ritual scene which first appeared in *The Eagle of the Ninth*, is built into a thrilling climax of darkness and light. The threat of the little grey dagger that flashes in the firelight, and the fear of the wolves gathering for the kill are memorable passages:

'Nearer and nearer, circling warily, came the grey leader, squirming and slinking low-bellied over the snow. In the last moment it seemed to Drem that he had known this wolf before; and the wolf had known him. The wicked grin, the welcome in the savage yellow eyes belonged to a before-time as well as to now. But then it had been the wolf who waited for the meeting. Now it was Drem!'

In this book there is also a certain heroic-comic relief in the Ajax-figure of Drem's grandfather, more rounded than Marcus' unapproachable uncle. He has the stubborn peevishness of the very old, and is an exasperating character, scarcely lovable, but instantly recognizable by the young.

'The grandfather was scowling at all of them under his thick grey-gold brows. "I am old, and it is not good for my belly that I do not have what I wish. What I wish is to be left in peace to enjoy myself, on this, the night that the youngest son of my youngest son becomes a man. The fire will burn for a long while yet, Woman, I shall remain here as long as I choose. . . ." '

Few of us who are concerned with the young can get as near to their inner lives as a writer can. The author is the ideal companion, Talore the great hunter, the wise one who understands. In this book, Miss Sutcliff makes her experience of the fire of trial clear to the reader, who recognizes its authenticity from its complete lack of sentimental self-regard. To win through to the desired place in the tribe, to be accepted as adult, as artist, one must fulfil the demands of the task in hand and forget oneself. Only thus does one develop integrity. This is as true for the author wrestling with his material as for the adolescent facing the future. In *Warrior Scarlet* they are fully and symbolically identified with each other.

Outside the scope of this essay are Miss Sutcliff's two adult novels, *Lady in Waiting* and *The Rider of the White Horse*, which must be judged in another place. In *Houses and History* published in 1960 Miss Sutcliff brings her skill as a novelist to bear on some of the intimate dramas of history in their settings. She catches fire where the details are such as she would have chosen for her own stories, but on the whole she seems straitened and too much at the mercy of her commission. Her admirers will recognize her response to the material, and she is entirely at home with the houses and their inhabitants, but there is an uneasy in-between-ness about this book, a kind of precocious worldliness from which the novels are entirely free, and, it must be admitted, a relapse in style.

'A labour of delight' is how Miss Sutcliff describes her writing of the monograph on Rudyard Kipling in this series. It has her childhood pleasure in this author in it, and despite all that has been written about Kipling, this short study succeeds in presenting a point of view as original as it is distinctive. Reviewers were quick to notice that it is 'a miniature in prose'. It has also the vision of the creative artist who prefers the selection of memorable details to a more academic judgment. Kipling has continuing popularity with children, and in this little book Miss Sutcliff shows that she is on the child's side. It is a significant tribute, and full of delight which seems as spontaneous now as it doubtless was when the little girl first heard the stories which were to inspire her own.

Despite all the abundance of children's books nowadays, there is still a need to tell the great tales again. To the Bodley Head library of heroic retellings Rosemary Sutcliff has contributed *Beowulf*. Here one can see how her visualizing power bodies forth the story as a sea drama. The heroes are seafarers, the threat is from the sea cave, the firedrake's hoard is under the Whale's Ness. The heroic outlines stand out as the result of economy in the telling which, despite omissions, gives a faithful account of the original. More important, the legend becomes immediately accessible to the young as a rousing tale of courage and magnanimity. In returning to one of the favourite tales of her childhood, Rosemary Sutcliff shares her delight in *Beowulf* with the next generation. Those who have read her other books will recognize her distinctive style. Here is the fight with the dragon:

'Fire was in his wings and a blasting flame leapt from his eyes. With wings spread, he half-flew, half-sprang at Beowulf, who stood firm to meet him and swung up his sword for a mighty blow. The bright blade flashed down, wounding the monster in the head: but though the skin gaped and the stinking blood sprang forth, the bones of the skull turned the blow so that the wound was not mortal. Bellowing, the creature crouched back, then sprang again, and Beowulf was wrapped from head to heel in a great cloud of fire. The iron rings of his mail seared him to the bone and the great shield of smith's work glowed red-hot as he strove to guard his face and bring up his blade for another blow.'

VI. Readers and Responses

Rosemary Sutcliff belongs to that small group of authors who write for children and not only cater for their taste but help to form it. Her concern to make each book reflect her vision of the theme means that she now never writes down to her readers as she came near to doing once or twice in the early novels. Instead she makes stringent demands on them. They are expected to grasp the topography of Roman Britain, the intricacies of life with the legions, the cross-country journeys and marches, and to respond to the subtleties of feeling in the writing. Sometimes they are swept along in a blaze of imagery or poised in a moment of suspense. Adult critics, who do not always realize the extent to which an adolescent feels his way into the heart of a situation or responds emotively to a climax in the story, accuse Miss Sutcliff of 'fine writing'. This is to miss the effectiveness of her most characteristic passages.

Even the most conscientious scholars fail to find fault with the details of the later novels, so that history teachers look to Miss Sutcliff to bridge the gap between history at the junior stage and what they call 'the real thing', which, presumably, means examinations. Indeed, they have discovered that as the shadow of the textbook grows longer it is the novelist who keeps alive the romance of history. While the facts are being mastered for reproduction, the novelist encourages the young to wonder what would have happened if things had been different,

66

if the legions had not been withdrawn to Rome, and in that wondering safeguards the pleasurable response to history.

When children discuss Miss Sutcliff's books with their teachers they are clear about the reasons for their enjoyment: the story grips them, they are involved in the fate of the characters and at the same time there is something that 'feels strange', especially in *The Shield Ring* and in *The Silver Branch*. They ask questions about the symbolic passages where the change to come is hinted at, about the first iron dagger, the altar to Mithras, the Christian symbols. While the questions seem matter-of-fact, the children are clearly responding to the 'felt' significance of the details.

Some reviewers have taken exception to the scenes of cruelty in *Outcast* and the fight at the king-making in *Warrior Scarlet*. Adults forget that although children are sensitive and subject to nightmares, more than cruelty they instinctively fear warped sadism or unnecessary violence, and these are not found in Miss Sutcliff. Certainly some historical novelists go too far, and parents and librarians become wary about which to recommend. There is no evidence to suggest that Miss Sutcliff's readers, who are, after all, often fourteen and over, suffer from her realistic descriptions.

Younger children write to ask about the fate of the characters they have come to know as friends. 'Was Beric happy in the Roman Army and did he find a nice wife?' There are the usual requests for sequels, especially about Marcus and Tamsyn.

One little girl wrote to say,.'I feel as though all the people in the book are my friends, and when I am in bed at night I pretend I'm talking to them'. Authors are wise nevertheless to consult their own preferences rather than those of their readers and to produce the next book in their own fashion.

Miss Sutcliff has a wide circle of older readers, mostly of young people whose time at school has gone on beyond the statutory leaving age, and some of her children's novels are in adult libraries. On one occasion an American Army captain in California, when he had read *The Eagle of the Ninth*, sent her a tune for the marching song. This adult interest is not surprising, for Miss Sutcliff counts on her readers possessing considerable competence and skill. She is a 'stretching' author.

This has led to the suggestion that she writes primarily for the bookish child. Librarians and her publishers dispute this, and certainly the books are seldom left for long on library shelves. Part of the great popularity of *The Eagle of the Ninth* may have come from the serial broadcasts of it in Children's Hour. It was repeated in its entirety at the children's request and one episode was given a third time in response to their demand. Librarians also say that it is difficult to predict which children will become enthusiastic readers of Miss Sutcliff. It seems that the initial difficulties are often got over when an enthusiastic teacher reads an episode in class, for some children experience difficulty in catching the 'tune' of a sophisticated novelist who is new to them. Once launched, they are carried along by the story-telling.

The essential Englishness in both theme and location suggests that Rosemary Sutcliff would find her public restricted, but this is by no means the case. Her publishers report that she is well-known in North America, where *The Shield Ring*, *Warrior Scarlet*, *The Lantern Bearers* and *Knight's Fee* were named Notable Children's Books by the American Library Association. Several books have been translated into German and the Scandinavian languages. There is also a version of *Warrior Scarlet* in Serbo-Croat.

During the last few years the historical novel has increased in popularity, scope and effectiveness. In this form of writing for children one can confidently say that the highest standards of artistry and craftsmanship prevail. Rosemary Sutcliff's work is characterized by a degree of intensity akin to poetic fervour. Her imaginative reconstruction of the past and the themes of heroic legend find an echo in the idealism of the modern adolescent. She combines great talent and industry with the incomparable gifts of the true story-teller. Praise for her work, simply because it is amongst the best of its kind, is bound to seem excessive, but the more exacting the criticism, the more favourable the final judgment must be.

Appendix

MISS SUTCLIFF'S

BIBLIOGRAPHY FOR 'THE LANTERN BEARERS'

Roman Britain, R. G. Collingwood
Pelican History of England, *Vol.* 1, I. A. Richmond
Social England, *Vol.* 1, H. D. Trail
The Battle for Britain in the 5th Century, T. Dayrell Reed
The Rise of Wessex
The Makers of the Realms, Sir Arthur Bryant
The Romans in Britain, Sir Bertram Windle
The Roman Era in Britain, John Warde
Wanderings in Roman Britain, Arthur Weigall
Wanderings in Anglo-Saxon Britain, Arthur Weigall
Everyday Life in Roman Britain, P. Quennell
Everyday Life in Saxon, Viking and Norman Times, P. Quennell
De Excidio Britanniae, Gildas
Historie Britannicus, Nennius
History of the Kings of Britain, Geoffrey of Monmouth
The History of the Kings of England, William of Malmesbury
Myths and Legends of the Celtic Race, Rolleston
Nineteen Centuries of British Costume, E. J. Ashdown
A Short History of Costume and Armour, F. M. Kelly and R.
   Schwabe
British and Foreign Arms and Armour, C. H. Ashdown
The Story of the Nations, Wales
Roman Frontiers in Wales, Nash and Williams
Royal Commission on Ancient Monuments—Caernarvonshire
Description of Caernarvonshire, Hall
The Heart of North Wales, Lowe
Mountains of Snowdonia, H. R. C. Carr and G. A. Lister
Caernarvonshire Historical Society Transactions, 1956
Segontium and the Roman Occupation of Wales, Sir Mortimer
   Wheeler
Welsh Christianity, A. W. Wade-Evans
Bartholomew's Relief maps of Snowdonia, Hants and Wilts, and
   various others on Jutland, Celtic Christianity and monasti-
   cism

BIBLIOGRAPHY

The Chronicles of Robin Hood, Oxford University Press, 1950.
Reprinted 1955, 1961
The Queen Elizabeth Story, Oxford University Press, 1950.
Reprinted 1952, 1958 (Oxford Children's Library edn.)
The Armourer's House, Oxford University Press, 1951. Reprinted
1957
Brother Dusty-Feet, Oxford University Press, 1952. Reprinted
1959 (Oxford Children's Library edn.)
Simon, Oxford University Press, 1953. Reprinted 1959 (Oxford
Children's Library edn.)
The Eagle of the Ninth, Oxford University Press, 1954. Reprinted
1955, 1957, 1959, 1961
Outcast, Oxford University Press, 1955. Reprinted 1957, 1959
The Shield Ring, Oxford University Press, 1956. Reprinted 1957,
1960
The Silver Branch, Oxford University Press, 1957. Reprinted 1959
Warrior Scarlet, Oxford University Press, 1958. Reprinted 1959
The Lantern Bearers, Oxford University Press, 1959. Reprinted
1961
The Bridge Builders, Basil Blackwell, 1959
Knight's Fee, Oxford University Press, 1960. Reprinted 1961
Houses and History, Batsford, 1960
Rudyard Kipling, The Bodley Head, 1960
Dawn Wind, Oxford University Press, 1961
Beowulf, The Bodley Head, 1961

and two adult novels:
Lady in Waiting, Hodder, 1956
The Rider of the White Horse, Hodder, 1959

AMERICAN EDITIONS

The Armourer's House, Henry Z. Walck, Inc., 1952
Brother Dusty-Feet, Henry Z. Walck, Inc., 1953
The Chronicles of Robin Hood, Henry Z. Walck, Inc., 1953
Simon, Henry Z. Walck, Inc., 1953
The Eagle of the Ninth, Henry Z. Walck, Inc., 1954
Outcast, Henry Z. Walck, Inc., 1955
The Shield Ring, Henry Z. Walck, Inc., 1957

The Silver Branch, Henry Z. Walck, Inc., 1958
Warrior Scarlet, Henry Z. Walck, Inc., 1958
The Lantern Bearers, Henry Z. Walck, Inc., 1959
Knight's Fee, Henry Z. Walck, Inc., 1960
Rudyard Kipling, Henry Z. Walck, Inc., 1961
Dawn Wind, Henry Z. Walck, Inc., 1962
Beowulf, E. P. Dutton & Co., Inc., 1962

and an adult novel:
Rider on a White Horse, Coward-McCann, Inc., 1959

MARYGROVE COLLEGE

3 1927 00077237 3

DATE DUE

GAYLORD			PRINTED IN U

Printed in the USA
CPSIA information can be obtained
at www.ICGtesting.com
LVHW020247141023
761039LV00004B/304